An Analysis Of Schiller's Tragedy, Die Brant Von Messina After Aristotle's Poetic: Inaugural Dissertation ... At The Georgia Augusta University In Göttingen

Isaac Flagg

AN

ANALYSIS

OF

SCHILLER'S TRAGEDY,

Die Braut von Messina,

AFTER

ARISTOTLE'S POETIC.

...... παράδειγμ' ἔχων
τὸν σὸν δαίμονα, τὸν σόν, ὦ
τλάμων Ὀιδιπόδα ....

SOPHOCLES.

INAUGURAL DISSERTATION

FOR OBTAINING THE DEGREE OF

DOCTOR OF PHILOSOPHY

AT THE

GEORGIA AUGUSTA UNIVERSITY IN GÖTTINGEN

BY

ISAAC FLAGG,

OF CAMBRIDGE, MASSACHUSETTS,

UNITED STATES OF AMERICA.

GÖTTINGEN,

PRINTED AT THE UNIVERSITY PRESS BY E. A. HUTH.

1871.

Die Braut von Messina.

The drama of Schiller entitled *The Bride of Messina or The Hostile Brothers* is a professed imitation of the ancient Athenian tragedy. It attempts to reproduce in the German language an extinct dramatic form and spirit which the relics of Greek literature have in a few models preserved to memory. Equipped with a chorus it wears a veritable antique costume, standing alone among modern literary productions in this completeness of classic attire. Yet while scholars discover in *The Bride of Messina* a late born sister of the tragedies of Æschylus and Sophocles, the imitation is so happily merged in the originality of the imitator, who has contrived to enliven the gray shapes of the past by casting on them a light suited to the modern eye, that the unlearned reader finds in this drama an impressive work of creative genius, — the best evidence of success in the treatment of an art whose laws sprang fresh from nature and are valid for all time. The purpose of this essay is to analyze the play, to show its realization of the antique ideal, and to note individual points of similarity or of unessential variance between it and the extant Greek tragedies.

The first clear insight into the distinguishing peculiarities of the Attic tragic art is gained through direct

1

perusal of its few remaining specimens, assisted by an acquaintance with the historical conditions that affected the growth of that branch of intellectual activity. Especial aid to aesthetic judgment is rendered by Aristotle's treatise on poetry, which, although it lies before us in a disarranged and abbreviated form, contains the headings of an acute and instructive course of thought. The most interesting observations in this treatise are those upon tragedy, which the philosopher regards as superior to epic poetry (XXVI) *, while he further declares his choice among the existing varieties of the tragic species itself. A broader range of investigation and selection was open to Aristotle in this field than is now offered in the fragment of Greek dramatic literature that has been saved; yet the two plays to which he most frequently refers as models are still extant and adequately illustrate his preferences. / After defining tragedy he proceeds to enumerate its specific parts, and names first the μῦθος or *plot*, using the word here in a technical sense, and defining it by the phrase σύνθε-σις τῶν πραγμάτων or *the contexture of incidents*. To the plot he assigns so emphatically the chief importance among the parts as to declare that it is the *soul* of tragedy (VI). He classifies the works of the tragic poets with reference to their resemblances in its treatment, and awards the prize to those whose plots are the most artistically constructed. It is true that of the extant tragedies only a few contain an elaborate plot; that a large majority and some of the best of them are extremely simple or even defective in this regard: we shall nevertheless be disposed to justify in the main the predilections of the philosopher, on observing how well a good plot, as understood by him, is suited to display to their best advantage the peculiarities

* The Roman numbers in parentheses throughout the dissertation refer to the chapters of Aristotle's *Poetic*.

of the ancient drama, and how thoroughly consistent
elaborateness in the formation of this part is with perfection of the others deemed by him of secondary importance. It is in their connection with the plot that Aristotle treats of the completeness and unity, and of other
essential properties, of a tragedy; with reference to this
part he comes to discuss the characters and their mutual
relations, and the effects of certain situations on the mind
of the beholder: it is, in short, a plan determining the
contour of the dramatic edifice, which becomes a shapely
whole only through its aid. I intend, therefore, in studying
the play before us, to use its plot as a nucleus around
which to group the treatment of subjects that naturally
grow out of it, since such a method will confine us to
discussions strictly appropriate to the ends proposed.
Moreover, it is in the contexture of incidents that the
poet of *The Bride of Messina* has most conspicuously displayed his skill in reviving the antique spirit, thus tacitly
assenting to the judgment of Aristotle, and rendering the
piece a companion to the philosopher's favourites, the *King
Oedipus* of Sophocles and the *Iphigeneia at Tauri* of Euripides.

Before examining the μῦϑος in the technical sense
above described, it will be well to survey the fiction that
underlies this tragedy in its general outlines, — the mythus
in its usual and wider signification of myth or fable.
These outlines are in every Greek play so traced upon its
own scenes as to convey to the spectator without further
assistance all information requisite to a distinct understand-
ing of the action represented; a violation of this principle
of self-sufficient wholeness would be a flagrant offence
against the rules of antique tragic composition. The pages
of our poem, therefore, the only source we are at liberty
to approach, furnish alone the story of which I here give

a brief comprehensive sketch. The sovereigns of Messina, belonging to a hardier and sterner stock, came in former time from the west by sea, subjecting the feebler race and protecting it against hostile neighbours. A prince of this line had possessed himself by violence of the bride designed by his father as his own. The outraged parent curses the unrighteous union, and from it spring two sons, the hostile brothers, from infancy estranged by mutual hatred. Their father, disturbed by a strange dream, on applying to a magian for its interpretation, is informed that, if a daughter should be born to him, *she would kill both his sons and annihilate his race*. A daughter *is* born, an order is given by the father to cast the infant into the sea, but the mother, to whom another oracle had foretold that a daughter *should unite in ardent love the conflicting hearts of her sons*, rescues the newly born with the aid of a trusty servant, and the girl is reared secretly and in ignorance of her parentage within a retired cloister. The resemblance of this fiction to the famous Theban legend which has furnished the themes of five extant Greek tragedies is at once apparent. The abduction of his bride calls forth the curses of the prince of Messina, as the rape of the boy Chrysippus by Laius provoked Pelops' imprecations on the Theban house; and the offender in the present story, warned, like Laius, of ruinous consequences to follow the birth of offspring, attempts to thwart the divine decree by assigning his child to the waves, as the infant Œdipus was exposed on Mount Cithaeron; while the hostile brothers are the counterparts of the unhappy sons of Œdipus, Eteocles and Polyneices. The poet has transferred from ancient fable those internal characteristics which, as will appear, would alone enable him to reproduce the peculiar religious spirit that pervaded Greek dramatic representation; but in quest of a fresher exterior he has passed beyond the boundaries of the Hellenic mythology into a new scene and among different surroundings. This is, indeed, a departure from the usual practice of the ancient Greeks, who with rare exceptions limited both poetic and plastic art to the province of their mythical religion, but it violates no essential principle. For such a step both authority and precedent are furnished by the treatise on poetry: for there we read (IX) that a poet need not confine himself to the traditional subjects of tragedy, which would be a ridiculous restraint, but may invent freely in the composition of a play; and a tragedy of Agatho, called *The Flower,* is mentioned with commendation, in which both names and occurrences were fictitious.

Passing to the mythus in its narrower signification, we find that the plot of the play before us belongs to the sort termed by Aristotle *involved* (πεπλεγμένος), which differs from the *simple* (ἁπλοῦς) sort in that the issue is brought about in the former with a *revolution* or with a *discovery* or with both, while the simple sort is destitute of these (X). Further, he divides every tragedy into two parts, the *complication* and the *development;* the former includes all of the action up to the point where the revolution begins, the latter all the rest of the play (XVIII). It remains to examine these divisions in their natural order.

I. The Complication (δέσις).

The δέσις, says Aristotle, embraces those events that lie outside the action represented, and some of those that are within it. The arrangement of the plot renders it convenient to consider first

(a) *The Events within the Action* (τὰ ἔσωθεν).

The *prologus* * begins with an harangue of Donna Isabella, the widowed princess of Messina, mother of the hostile brothers, to the elders of the city, who have been summoned to the palace. The address apprises the spectator of the occasion of the assembly and the princess' appearance before it. A friendly meeting of the sons, for the first time since their father's decease three months previously, has been appointed for this day, and the elders are commanded to prepare for a respectful reception of their lords. The tone of the speaker is at once an imperious and a reproachful one, and the latter feeling is explained by allusions the princess makes to recent occurrences. The hatred of the brothers, forcibly restrained from outbreak by their father until his death, had, immediately after that event, burst into a conflict through which Messina became divided against itself, siding with the one or the other of the princes. The already distressed mother, harshly censured by the elders for the public misfortunes occasioned by her sons' strife, had thrown herself between the combatants, whose only bond of sympathy was their love for her, and by dint of tears and entreaty had gained their consent to a peaceful meeting in the paternal castle.

The prologus is thus made a part of the plot, and is not begun, as in the plays of Euripides, with a direct introductory speech equally unaccounted for and unconnected

---

* Πρόλογος is the term applied to the whole of that part of a tragedy which precedes the πάροδος or entrance - chant of the chorus: for the parts included between songs of the entire chorus the technical name is ἐπεισόδιον, for the songs themselves στάσιμον; while the last part, having no choral ode after it, is called ἔξοδος (XII).

with the action. However necessary it may be to give the spectator at the outset of a drama information concerning the posture of events, this, to preserve unity and symmetry, must be conveyed indirectly through the natural course of the dramatic imitation, as in the scene just analyzed. Hence the passage is properly to be reckoned among the parts of the complication lying *within* the action, although previous events are touched upon and are made known by it; for to the representation the assembly and the harangue were of primary, the allusions of secondary, importance. That the princess should recount before the elders facts of which they are already aware is natural, since such explicitness is prompted by, and serves to give force to, the indignation with which she rebukes them for the selfish and heartless demeanour they had manifested. In the opening scene of the *Oedipus* of Sophocles, where the priest upon inquiry by the king explains the purpose of the suppliant gathering and describes at length the wretched plight of the plague-visited city, — things already known to the inquirer (γνωτὰ κοὐκ ἄγνωτά μοι, v. 58), — the explicitness, while it instructs the audience indirectly, is called for by the earnestness of the situation and lends pathos to the prayer for aid. The tragedies of Euripides, on the contrary, open with monologues, which, even when in themselves to be accounted for, contain recitals of details only attributable to the poet's design of advising the spectator. Comprising matter that the law of completeness renders indispensable, such passages exhibit as an excrescence attached to the surface of the plot what ought to be assimilated to its heart and fibre. They suggest the modern prologue, and make up one among several symptoms in Euripides' works of a tendency toward the creation of a new dramatic species, — a growth in which the young germs of the poet's genius were stunted by traditional restrictions from which he could not free himself. His plays betray the defects and suffer the disadvantages invariably attendant upon a transitional condition, wherein that which may be commended from one point of view as advancement can from the opposite side be regarded only as degeneration. Of the tragedies of Sophocles, which represent the perfection of the unmixed antique style, there is one extant, the *Women of Trachis*, that exhibits the fault just considered. For there, although the arrival of the day designated by the oracle as decisive of the fate of Hercules offers a starting point for the action and explains the anxiety of his consort Deianeira, yet the preponderance of the narrative element in her soliloquy, — her circumstantial review of facts in her life's history, — is but inadequately justified even by that natural impulse which gave rise to the custom of repeating a tale of sorrow in solitude to the elements, as if to seek consolation from the sympathy of higher powers. This psychological truth serves more appropriately as a motive for *songs from the stage* (τὰ ἀπὸ τῆς σκηνῆς, XII), where a mental state is mainly to be represented and the lyric tone outweighs the epic. *

The elders having withdrawn in deferential silence, Donna Isabella beckons to Diego, an aged attendant, and reminding him, after a word of commendation for his long tested fidelity in a clandestine service, that the day has arrived for her secret to be revealed, bids him repair to the cloister to bring home the treasure long since intrusted to its keeping. As he goes, the mother hears the clang

---

* Examples are: — Aesch. *Prom.* vv. 88—127; Soph. *El.* vv. 86—120; Eur. *Andr.* vv. 91—116. In the passage last cited Andromache, in a manner characteristic of Euripides, is made to give the philosophical explanation of her conduct; compare Eur. *Med.* vv. 56—58.

of trumpets nearing from either side, and hastens from the scene to receive her sons. This passage forms a sort of second part of the prologus, marking an instant at which the slowly turning wheels of the dramatic machinery acquire their full velocity and momentum. With Euripides the play itself first properly begins with this second part, after the conclusion of his prelude; but illustrations of the manner above described are to be found in the works of the other poets, (as in the *Oedipus* the arrival of Creon from Delphi, with the consequent order of the king to assemble the Cadmeans, denotes this point of accelerated motion)

The entrance of the chorus and its performance of the *parodus* ensue. Reflections upon the nature of the chorus, and upon the relations between its odes and the leading precepts of the tragic lesson, will connect themselves appropriately with later portions of the analysis; for the present we have to deal only with the immediate participation of the chorus in the action, and with such lyric passages as touch directly the course of events. Suffice it here to state that the chorus in *The Bride of Messina* is a double one, each semichorus being composed of knights in the retinue of one of the princes; that in their difference of years the ages of their respective lords are mirrored; while the fraternal discord is suggested here at the outset by their entrance from opposite sides of the *orchestra*. The first *episodium* is introduced by the appearance of the princess with her sons, greeted by the closing words in the choral chant, and begins with the scene of *reconciliation*. The passage may be instructively studied through a comparison of it with that in Euripides' *Phoenissae* (vv. 443 —637), where Jocasta brings together her estranged sons, Eteocles and Polyneices, with the same design of effecting harmony between them. In respect of details the scenes in the two plays present a marked contrast, the varying modes of treatment arising principally from the unlike conceptions of the origin of the fraternal enmity in the respective legends. In the Greek fable the hostility was produced through the brothers' own efforts to avoid the estrangement invoked upon them by the curse of Œdipus*; in our story the mutual hatred is an inborn one, a direct result of the grandfather's imprecations. The origin of the dissension in the former case is an illustration of tragic irony (a term that will be explained hereafter); in the latter the irony is exemplified rather in the reconciliation itself, which leads to consequences the reverse of those intended. Accordingly the attempt at mediation, unsuccessful in the ancient play, here meets with success and forms an important part of the *complication*. The diversity in the modes of viewing the hostility will sufficiently explain the absence in the present passage of the judicial formality and display of disputatious skill conspicuous in the corresponding scene of the *Phoenissae*, although the good judgment of the poet would have forbidden his imitating under any circumstances this peculiarity of the Attic drama. Here, as each son claims to be heard in his defence, both are put off by the mother, who will admit no distinction between offender and offended in a feud that dates from unthinking childhood; in the play of Euripides, on the other hand, there is really a case, and the brothers are called upon to plead their respective causes, Polyneices as the aggrieved party and accuser taking the lead. A contest in dialectics is thus as appropriate, relatively considered, to the one of the situations as it were unsuitable for the other, while from the standpoint of absolute taste the overstrained subtlety in argumentation that marks many tedious debates in the Greek dramatic poetry can

---

* Eur. *Phoen.* vv. 66—80, in the *prologue*.

be regarded only as a disfigurement to any tragedy. The litigious disposition of the Athenians could not fail to imprint itself upon the literature whose bloom was simultaneous with that of their political freedom and supremacy, the rise of sophistic inquiry and the spread of instruction in technical rhetoric lending weight to make the impression more distinct than ever upon the works of the youngest and most speculative of the three tragic masters. If we consider withal the extreme simplicity of form in the majority of Greek plays, itself a temptation to diffuseness both in debative and narrative passages, the phenomenon is explained and the fault extenuated.

The rhetorical element, however, has not been neglected by our poet, but appears, confined within due limits, in the hortatory address of the princess. Hence there is a greater similarity between the attitudes of the mothers in the scenes compared: both Jocasta and Donna Isabella are moved by an impartial affection for their alienated children; and the appeal of the latter against the perverseness of her sons' blind hostility evinces no less prudence and sagacity than we find displayed by the former in rebuking Eteocles' selfish defence of his injustice and in reprehending the cruel attempt in arms made by Polyneices against his native city. In the *Phoenissae* the queen remains to await the issue of her undertaking; but in the play before us the princess, irritated at the unbroken silence maintained by the brothers toward one another, leaves them after a short despairing apostrophe in which she ironically invokes upon them the bitter consequences of their infatuate strife. The remainder of the passage forms again a complete contrast to the conclusion of that in Euripides' piece. There the dialogue, passing from the iambic to the brisker trochaic rhythm, becomes warmer and angrier, until the sons of Œdipus part with mutual anathemas, to meet again only in deadly conflict. Here the discourse warms with a more genial fire, as each brother draws from the other's cautious overtures a recognition of the magnanimity that underlies the dispositions of both; and the reasonableness of the mother's words thus growing clearer upon their minds, the reconciliation becomes in a natural manner gradually complete. At the moment when its consummation is fully effected, a messenger enters, a spy previously sent out by Don Cesar the younger of the princes, as is learned from the words of the second semichorus, which announces his approach. He reports that *she who was lost and had been sought, is found and is not far distant.* To the inquiry *where,* he replies with the indefiniteness characteristic of the common man, and conscious of his importance as holder and withholder of valuable knowledge, that it is *here in Messina* that she hides herself. Don Cesar bids the messenger lead him to the place, and with a friendly word to his brother is about to depart, yet, feeling the impropriety of a hasty leave-taking at such a time, he returns to excuse his departure and to reiterate his expressions of sincerity in the new friendship. Then, after a formal declaration to the chorus of the truce that is henceforth to be observed alike by followers and followed, he withdraws accompanied by his semichorus. Here begins a passage to be treated in the next section under events outside the action, — the narration by Don Manuel, the elder brother, of the adventure that had led to his love for her whom he has designed in secret as his bride. It is his purpose now to divulge the secret, and he orders his retainers to make preparations for a pompous escort of the new princess to the palace. He selects two from the chorus to assist in supplying more immediate wants, and departs, enjoining secrecy upon the others, who remain in the *orchestra* and sing the first *stasimum*.

(b) *The Events outside the Action* (τὰ ἔξωϑεν).

All the events outside the action proper of a tragedy, being prior to it in time, must belong to the *complication,* and can only be described, not represented. Some of these have been mentioned in the previous section, where it seemed reasonable to treat them on account of the indirectness with which they were presented and their subordination to an important scene of the action imitated. Those now to be glanced at are given for the most part in the form of detailed narrations between persons in the play, and constitute the epic portion of the tragedy. The prominence of the descriptive element in Greek dramatic representation is one of the most obvious among the features distinguishing the ancient from the modern stage. The brief duration to which the assumed time of the action proper was restricted, — usually that of a single revolution of the sun (V), — combined with the striving after completeness and self-sufficiency in a drama, occasioned those descriptions which brought to light important events prior to the period represented. On the other hand, the distaste of the Greeks for the visible imitation of violent and atrocious acts, arising from a distrust in the tragic power of mere ocular illusion, with their fine susceptibility to the influences that work upon the imagination of intellect, caused narration, as a rule, to take the place of representation even in setting forth the most important deeds that fell within the limited action of the piece. Hence few plays are, like the *Ajax* of Sophocles, without elaborate and spirited epic passages either in the complication or the development; while some, as the *Iphigeneia at Tauri*, have narrations of both sorts. In *The Bride of*

Messina they are confined to the complication, since the disasters of the piece are represented upon the stage contrary to the ancient custom.

The first narration is given by Don Manuel to the semichorus of his followers, who have observed in their master during the parley of the brothers a distraction and apparent indifference unusual with him and unmeet to the occasion, and who now inquire the reason for this on the departure of Don Cesar. In reply he relates how on a hunting excursion shortly before his father's death the pursuit of a fawn had enticed him to the gate of a distant cloister into the presence of a maiden whose pet the creature proved to be, and who, though bound by no vow, was living within the cloister's walls; that he had concealed their mutual love from all until now, and had neither made known his station to the virgin nor taken pains to discover hers, of which she was herself ignorant, lest a disclosure might frustrate their plans of union; but that, since on the day before the present the old attendant who alone passed between the girl and her mysterious family had threatened for the morrow a revelation of her destiny, he had forestalled the possibility of an interruption of his designs by removing her furtively to a lonely garden in Messina, where she was now awaiting him and whence he will conduct her as bride to the palace. Another narration belonging to the complication is given in the third episodium, after the development has begun (an inversion of order that will be explained in another place), by Don Cesar in the presence of his mother and Don Manuel. The princess, awaiting the return of Diego with the treasure for which he was dispatched, has just informed her sons, united at last in feeling, of the existence of a younger sister, and has related the two oracles that had induced the father to expose his child and the mother to preserve it without his knowledge. Their surprise at learning this is equalled by hers at the announcements they have to make in their turn. Don Manuel reveals his design of leading home a bride this day, deferring with his cautious reserve an account of the circumstances. The younger and more impulsive brother declares a similar purpose and gives the history of his adventure. The princes had attended the funeral ceremony of their father, apart in the throng of mourners and disguised from one another, lest a quarrel might violate the reigning sanctity. Here Don Cesar, not unmindful of the earnestness of the situation, had beheld by his side one whom, though he knew not her birth and rank, the first glance had recognized as worthy to be a prince's choice. That the beloved of Don Cesar is the sister, is intimated to the spectator through her own words in the monody that opens the second episodium, and confirmed in the third by the confession of Diego on his return without her from the cloister; he had yielded to her entreaties to be allowed to attend the burial of the prince of Messina, believing that he recognized the divine will in the irresistible impulse that attracted the daughter to the father's grave. The original crime of the family, the offence of the deceased prince against his parent, is made known in the first stasimum of the chorus.

The importance of maintaining a show of probability in the plot of a tragedy is emphasized by Aristotle, who condemns those plays in which the incidents happen without apparent connection of cause and effect, adding that, if anything improbable must be introduced, it ought to be among the parts lying outside the action. It is obvious that the spectator would be involuntarily more indifferent and less vigilant regarding an unlikelihood in what is described or alluded to as past than toward the same in an event moving slowly before his eye. Aristotle cites in illustration his favourite Sophoclean tragedy, referring to the ignorance of Œdipus about the manner of Laius' death as an incredible assumption (XV. XXIV). He remarks that the supernatural also should be introduced only with reference to what is extraneous to the drama, and censures the *deus ex machina* as means of solving difficulties; here the *Iphigeneia at Tauri* might be cited, in which the rescue of Iphigeneia by Artemis from sacrifice is prior to the action represented. The plot of our tragedy conforms to these directions of the philosopher. The incidents within the action will be shown to contain no improbability, but to ensue according to necessary or likely consequence; but among the events of previous occurrence, presented in the narrative form, are some of which the improbability would betray itself in a detailed representation. Such is the fact that Don Manuel had never come into contact with his mother's servant Diego in his visits to the cloister; while the history of the fraternal discord and the motive assumed to account for the sister's attendance at the funeral verge on the supernatural. Oracles foretelling future events have their place, likewise, in the background, and they are accordingly in this play, as in the *Oedipus,* not promulgated until their truth has been already sufficiently attested by the course of events witnessed. Thus have the improbabilities been shaded by natural grouping and withdrawn from the observation of the impassioned beholder.

The mode of viewing the passion of love in the scenes above surveyed and in some of the later ones of the play is a noticeable variation from that exhibited in the antique models. In the ancient drama love, if introduced at all, held usually a subordinate position among other motives, or, when of especial prominence as in the *Hippolytus* of Euripides, assumed the form of a wonderful and resistless instinct, the province of a potent divinity in the religion

of nature. In modern literature the same passion, passed
through the clarifying influences of the age of chivalry,
appears as a refined sentiment, ennobled and armed with
new powers, and suited to be the leading motive in the
poetry of an enlightened people. The reader of *The Bride
of Messina* will note also the sense of knightly honour
displayed in the parley of reconciliation as a further characteristic of the period in which the scene of this drama
is laid. With the many praiseworthy and admirable traits
that distinguished the Grecian character, these gentler
sentiments are seldom found drawn upon the pages of the
Attic dramatic literature. All the more interesting and
estimable are the few instances in which such lineaments
are turned with a stronger light toward us; as in the
Philoctetes, where the magnanimity of Neoptolemus, son
of the most chivalrous of the mythical heroes, is portrayed,
and in the *Iphigeneia at Aulis*, which pictures Achilles'
own attitude before the daughter of Agamemnon.

II. The Development (λύσις).

Aristotle's division of every tragedy into complication
and development is one that applies to the incidents of
the fable in their actual temporal sequence, without regard to
their arrangement in the plot and the order in which they
are made known to actor or beholder. The λύσις begins
at a crisis where all those events have *in point of fact*
occurred, whose consequences gradually unfolded present
the striking situations that tragedy aims to exhibit; yet
important parts of the complication, prior to the action
represented, may remain unknown until this crisis is passed, and be first communicated in the course of the development itself. The development of the present tragedy

2

begins with the second episodium; but the revelation by
the princess of the existence of a daughter, and Don Cesar's
description of the funeral scene, are not introduced until
the third. So in the *Oedipus* the king's narration of his
journey from Corinth to the Delphic oracle and of his
rencounter with the unknown Laius does not come until
the development has set in.* Such an inversion of order
suits especially a plot containing revolution and discoveries,
since these forbid an early acquaintance on the part of
the acting persons with all the events of the complication,
while a partial ignorance on the side of the spectator
likewise is not without advantages. Plots of this kind
are, therefore, aptly termed by Aristotle *involved* and rightly
ranked as superior in tragic power to the simple sort,
other things being equal. For besides producing other
effects that will be noticed in the separate treatment of
the revolution and the discoveries, they are the best adapted
to increase suspense; but suspense engenders a nearer self-
identification with the participants in the action, and through
such sympathy we are rendered more susceptible to the
emotions of pity and terror, which Aristotle maintains it
is the office of tragedy to excite. While, therefore, the
spectator ought to know more of the state of events than
the acting persons, his emotions would be weakened by
learning too soon their real condition and certain issue.
At the end of our first episodium, where the complication
has reached its height, the beholder has gained a dim insight into mysteries that have not yet dawned upon the
characters themselves; he suspects that Diego the messenger
of the princess, Don Cesar ominously interrupting the
brotherly converse, Don Manuel intent upon bridal pomp,

* Soph. *Oed. Tyr.* vv. 771—833. The turning point is at v.
716; compare vv. 726—730.

are travelling upon convergent paths, and he dreads a collision like that at the triple cross-roads of Phocis: but he acquires a full comprehension of the fatal entanglement not till its consequences have in part been witnessed. The reader of the *Oedipus*, after hearing the king's solemn execration of the author of the pestilence, the unknown murderer, begins to dread from the demeanour of the seer Teiresias that the curse is to descend on him who uttered it: but the truth is first revealed through Œdipus' narration, after he has himself begun to perceive dimly that he is thus ensnared.

Consistent with the division into complication and development is the definition of *wholeness* given by the philosopher. A whole, he affirms, is that which has a beginning, a middle, and an end, a middle being that which implies of necessity that something has preceded, and requires that something else shall follow it (VII). Aristotle clearly intends to designate here the point which, in a piece of composition having the entireness and unity demanded by the laws of the Greek tragedy, marks the turn from complication to development. At this crisis an apparent suspension of the action often takes place, — a pause at the turning point of fortune, serving to prolong suspense and affording time for the dramatic elements to mingle preparatory to their reactionary effort. Such a pause is formed by the passage in the *Women of Trachis* where Deianeira declares her misgivings concerning the nature of the supposed love-potion she has sent Hercules; in the *Medea* by the wavering of the mother between love for her children and the resolve to slay them, after the deadly gifts have been presented to her rival: the *Choephoroe* is remarkable for an unusual prolongation of this oppressive hesitancy and delay, but an explanation is suggested by the position of the play as the middle one in a trilogy with

2*

affinity of themes. This period of suspended motion is occupied in the tragedy before us by a soliloquy of Beatrice, the sister and beloved of the princes, who is awaiting Don Manuel in the lonely garden to which she has fled with him from the cloister. The passage is, further, an example of songs from the stage, being emotional rather than narrative, although information is indirectly conveyed by it, and representing a conflict in which hope and contented resignation triumph over anxiety and remorse.*

In assigning to the plot the position of first importance among the constituents of tragedy, and in preferring the involved to the simple kind, Aristotle urges that to the plot belong *revolutions* and *discoveries*, the chief means by which tragedy captivates the soul.** He mentions elsewhere (XI) as a third part the *calamities*. Of these three parts, belonging necessarily to the *development*, it will be convenient first to treat

(a) The Discoveries (ἀναγνωρίσεις).

The word ἀναγνώρισις as employed in the treatise on poetry retains its usual signification of a change from ignorance to knowledge either concerning things and events or between persons about each other; but the philosopher discusses in detail discoveries of persons only, deeming these to be of highest importance to the plot and action, because most productive of pity and fear. The best discovery, he remarks, is one that takes place together with a revolution or change of fortune, as in the *Oedipus;* and it occurs in the best manner, when effected through the circumstances of the action itself with an appearance of probability, as in the play just mentioned and in the *Iphigeneia* (XI). As the discoveries in *The Bride of*

* See *Appendix, Version* I.
** τὰ μέγιστα οἷς ψυχαγωγεῖ ἡ τραγῳδία (VI).

Messina meet the requisitions prescribed, it is needless to recount here the other inferior sorts and methods cited by Aristotle from the works of the poets (XVI). Since, therefore, the discoveries in a tragedy are, when most artistically presented, inseparably interwoven with the whole network of the plot, I shall take occasion, in analyzing those of the present play, to give once for all a summary of the course of events, in order to render intelligible without repetition other discussions that are to follow. Hence the discoveries of facts will claim our attention as well as those of persons, and in this connexion the best opportunity will be afforded of showing how the *probability* requisite in the consecution of dramatic incidents has been attained. For as ignorance and error are the principal agents in furthering the complication of affairs, while discoveries help to precipitate the revolution, it is evident that, to give the plot a proper *duration* and render it sufficiently *involved,* the discoveries must be deferred until the right moment in the developing period. To achieve this avoidance and postponement of recognitions artistically, that is, with an appearance of probability and causation throughout, is the poet's first duty, and success therein a test of genius.

When the messenger arrived at the moment of reconciliation between the brothers with his report of having found her that was lost, an exact statement of the locality would have betrayed the state of matters to Don Manuel and thus have foiled the plan of complication; but such a disturbance is prevented by the verbose indefiniteness of the spy's account and answer, which is suited to his pretensions in possession of a weighty secret, and characteristic in general of the man of low degree, — a trait amply illustrated in the Greek tragedies. Again, as Don Cesar seems to be on the point of explaining hesitatingly the purpose of his haste, the elder brother, though disconcerted by the sudden departure at such a time, is all the more earnest in deprecating the offer to confide a secret, zealous to attest his sincerity in the new friendship, and absorbed, moreover, in a secret of his own. Here, then, the avoidance of untimely discovery is dexterously achieved through an appeal to psychological truth, illustrating a kind of probability that Aristotle in his treatment of *character* (XV) urges as of the utmost moment. Furthermore, the finding of the girl by the spy, and his consequent arrival to summon his master, have naturally taken place. For the prince, since the occurrence at his father's burial, had posted spies in every place where maiden innocence might show itself; and this one had seen Beatrice in a church adjoining the garden, whither she had ventured from her solitary hiding-place, hearing the call to prayer, and instinctively tempted to mind the summons so often obeyed during her life at the cloister.

Don Manuel's narration to the chorus of his adventure, and the declaration of his plans, have been presented in examining the parts outside the action, and the reasons stated why the communication was naturally made at that period. The intimations of the attendant of Beatrice that her parentage should be on this day revealed had led the prince to remove her from the cloister, while the disclosure to his followers is necessary, in order that they may be ready for the bridal escort. But had this recital occurred in the mother's presence, as that of the younger brother does, a premature discovery would have been the consequence. The reserve manifested by the elder son, both in his previous concealment of facts and in the brevity with which he now announces his purpose to the princess, belongs to his individuality and is remarked upon by the mother as a paternal trait.

Don Cesar, conducted to the garden by the spy, had entered the presence of the terrified maiden in place of the expected Don Manuel, and this is to be reckoned as the first event in the change of fortune. Declaring his name and the princely station to which he designs to exalt her as his consort, he mistakes the dismay betrayed in her countenance, as she discovers that the youth before whose glance she had trembled at the funeral service is one of the hostile brothers known to her by fame, for agitation at the prospect of sudden elevation in life; and leaving her, under guard of his retainers, to recover composure, he proceeds himself to the palace to announce his bride. The scene there, already described, is interrupted by the return of Diego without Beatrice, — an event foreseen by the spectator as a necessary consequence of what had been previously represented and narrated. (The inquiry of the princess, *Where is Beatrice?*, affects Don Manuel with disagreeable surprise through the identity of the name with that of his beloved: similarly in the *Oedipus* it is a single expression in Jocasta's story, — the mention of triple cross-roads, — that gives the king his first shock of fear lest Teiresias may have spoken truly in denouncing him as the murderer of Laius. Diego's allusion to a cloister arouses further fears in the lover's mind, while a statement that the sister has been kidnapped by corsairs affords relief: thus Œdipus is further alarmed by the coincidence of the time of Laius' death with that of his own adventure and by the similarity in age and number of attendants between the former king of Thebes and the stranger he had himself slain, but grasps at the hope afforded by a rumour that his predecessor had been killed by a band of robbers. But from the dialogue between Diego and Don Cesar it appears that the servant has no certain information concerning the manner of the sister's disappearance, and Don Manuel is still left in doubt. Then at the urgent appeal of the mother to both sons to search out and rescue their sister, the younger with characteristic impetuousness departs forthwith, while the elder lingers bewildered and attempts by questioning to arrive at certainty in respect of his apprehensions. Misunderstanding his behaviour and impatient at the delay, the princess indignantly again charges him to set forth, and to his anxious inquiry — *Pray in what region didst thou keep her hidden?* — rejoins petulantly: — *She were not more concealed beneath the earth.** In the *Iphigeneia,* as the two victims Orestes and Pylades stand before the priestess awaiting sacrifice, she asks which one is called Pylades (for this name had been overheard at their capture), and is informed; but when she further requests the other to give his name, Orestes, intent on preserving a manly composure before impending death, and loath to encourage what he deems to be a mistimed curiosity, answers: — *We should be called unlucky, by good right.*** Had he pronounced the name *Orestes,* a premature discovery would have ensued, as would have resulted from a definite reply to Don Manuel's question. At this moment Diego, recollecting Beatrice's visit to the funeral and suspecting that this may in some way have occasioned the loss, confesses that he allowed her to attend the ceremony in disguise: Don Manuel in thus again encouraged, since he had enjoined upon his mistress not to yield to this impulse; yet tortured by doubts he departs to assure himself from her own lips, just as his brother returns. We saw Don Cesar rush suddenly forth upon the errand of search as was consistent with his nature. Had he remained longer, he

---

* Verborgner nicht war sie im Schooß der Erde!

** τὸ μὲν δίκαιον δυστυχεῖς καλοίμεσϑ᾽ ἄν.

Eur. Iph. Taur. v. 500.

---

would have heard Diego's story and have made his discovery too soon: he has now returned to learn the locality of the cloister from which the sister was robbed, as a clew to guide him in the pursuit; and the information, sought with these motives, is readily given by Donna Isabella. Had Don Cesar made the inquiry in this manner at the outset, as a cooler head would not have failed to do, the revelation would have confirmed the misgivings of Don Manuel beyond dispute and again have thwarted the plan. By such delicate balancing of individual characteristic and consecution of incident has the poet been enabled to steer safely past these threatening points of danger.

As the followers of Don Manuel approach the garden with the bridal gifts, they find themselves barred from entrance by their former rivals, the knights of Don Cesar. The words that pass between the parties (given in the form of the *stichomythia* or brisk dialogue in alternate single verses) end, as each semichorus abides by the orders of its absent lord, in the drawing of swords. An actual conflict is prevented by the arrival of Don Manuel, who in surprise and anger at their hostile attitude steps between and demands an explanation from his own men; the others, upon this, out of respect for the new peace, to which he appeals, obey his command to withdraw. His discovery is still further delayed after joining Beatrice by her importunities to fly from danger. To quiet her fears he makes known to her for the first time his rank as prince of Messina. With increased suspicion at the sight of her consternation when she learns this, he begins his inquiries, first touching the mother, whom he regards as the prominent person in the question of identity; and his apprehensions are augmented by the description of her mother's features that Beatrice gives from an early reminiscence.

Words of Don Cesar are heard from behind the scenes, and Don Manuel, who observes that she recognizes the voice, combining instantly the narrative of his brother with Diego's confession, puts in despair the decisive question to Beatrice, whether she was present at the burial of his father; her answer, that she disobeyed his injunctions and went, makes certain her identity as his sister. Don Cesar, who had come to take away his bride before renewing the search for the lost sister, enters at this juncture under the guidance of his recently dismissed retainers, sees Beatrice clinging to Don Manuel, and in a burst of jealous rage and indignation at his brother's supposed deceit and treachery draws and deals him a fatal thrust, while Beatrice falls in a swoon. Another collision between the knights is hindered by Don Cesar; proclaiming the justice of his deed he warns off his brother's men, and bidding his own lend aid to the lifeless bride and convey her to his mother he departs to continue the pursuit. The remaining semichorus surrounds the body of its lord and chants a dirge.

The next discovery — by Beatrice of her own relationship — begins when her eyes, as she awakes in the palace from her swoon, meet the dimly remembered features of Donna Isabella, and the presence of Diego convinces her that the remembrance is trustworthy. Then relating in allusion to the recent scenes, which she believes to be a dream, how she had feared they would bring her to the mother of the hostile princes, she is informed by the princess that she beholds before her that mother and that they are her own brothers. Of the truth of this the girl is assured, as her eye wanders toward the knights, who had been ordered after depositing their senseless burden to draw back, that her first glance on awakening might fall upon her mother. This proof of the reality of her dream, combined with the words just heard from the princess, reveals in full to Beatrice her dire fate. Donna Isabella, startled at the horror shown by her daughter and at the restlessness of the chorus, is brought gradually from mere apprehension to a knowledge of the truth. She hears the tones of an approaching funeral march, the first semichorus enters bearing the corpse upon a bier, Beatrice removes the pall and exposes the murdered son. Overwhelmed with bitterness at this sight the mother, believing him to have been slain by robbers in the act of rescuing his sister from them, bursts into imprecations on the hand of the murderer, on her that bore him, and on his whole race. Reverting to the prophecies, which seem to be refuted by this event, she gives way to loud abuse of all oracles and the seer's art; as Jocasta, when the Corinthian herald reports the natural death of Œdipus' reputed father Polybus, thinking the Delphic oracle thus proved untrue, rails at the prophecies of the gods with impious contempt. Here the chorus in words of gloomy import announces the approach of Don Cesar. Welcomed by the unsuspecting mother as her only remaining son he shuns the subject of his brother's death and proceeds to report about the sister. Thereupon the princess expresses her thankfulness for the restoration of the lost one, and in so doing reveals to Don Cesar that his bride and his sister are identical. The fallacy of the justification he had imagined for the deed of violence becomes at the same instant manifest; in a frenzy of bitterness he curses the secrecy that had caused all these horrors, and now boldly proclaims, what he had as yet spared his mother, that he is the murderer of Don Manuel. The scene that ensues upon this consummation of discoveries presents a situation worthy to serve as an example of tragic art: a mother driven by despair to the extremity of impious scorn; a fratricide conscious of the enormity of his crime, pleading for a last and mournful consolation in the recognition of his equal claims with the dead to the affection of a sister robbed of a lover and brother by his hand.*

(b) The Revolution (περιπέτεια).

A περιπέτεια is defined to be a change to the reverse of what is intended by the course of action (XI). This change of fortune, if *single*, may be either from adverse to prosperous or from prosperous to adverse; if *double*, it ends with one issue for the good, and a contrary one for the bad, characters, as in the *Odyssey*. The last sort is condemned by Aristotle as more appropriate to comedy than to tragedy; while of the *single* kinds, although the word τραγῳδία did not signify exclusively a play of disastrous termination, yet he justly prefers the change from prosperity to adversity as best suited to produce the effects aimed at by the *ideal* tragedy (XIII). By the invention of a fable closely modelled after the Theban legend, represented through an *involved* plot with an elaborate *revolution* like that illustrated in the *King Oedipus* of Sophocles and prescribed by Aristotle, the modern poet has incorporated into his drama the fundamental religious idea of Greek tragedy with such thoroughness as completely to neutralize the unessential minor variations from the antique which he has with commendable boldness introduced. A belief in the inevitable retribution of crime, — in a *nemesis* worked out sooner or later in the family of a guilty person until the balance of righteous order and eternal justice in nature is restored, effected, too, not by direct interposition of divine power, but through the apparently free action of the sufferers themselves in accordance with the necessary laws of causation and conse-

* See *Appendix, Version* II.

quence; — this conviction it was the aim of the Æschylean and Sophoclean tragedy to justify and strengthen by its imitation of calamitous misfortune: and while, indeed, many of the plays that remain to us illustrate in the single actions that form their special themes but one page of the great lesson, the fullest scope for the satisfaction of this sentiment is afforded by the plot that artistically opens to view the whole course of a retributive change from an elevated prosperity tô complete ruin. Indispensable to the demands of this belief is the preservation of a consistent *probability* and appearance of causation in the sequence of events imitated, that the fixed ordinances of eternal right, not disturbing interposing powers, may seem to work out the recompense of crime; for the only divinities that may interfere are the *Erinyes*, typical of remorse, which goads the guilty to expiatory penance, and the infatuating *Ate,* with the tragedians but the personification of an inherent force in human temperaments that enables offended nature to recover her claims. To this end the *characters* of the acting persons must be adapted, that each may naturally adopt a procedure conducive to the required calamitous issue, and that their own frailty may seem to justify the fate which overtakes them, even though they be in part atoning for an ancestral crime. Nor should the characters in the drama be themselves unmindful of the righteous decrees which their history is exemplifying and before which they are to succumb, but the spectator should hear the law promulgated and applauded from the mouths of its victims. Here is the origin of that *tragic irony*, employed with marvellous power by the masters of the ancient art, whereby a phrase conveys to the audience a double signification or a deeper one than is intended by the speaker, suggesting a grave application to his own case. The ambiguous and seemingly conflicting oracles of

Grecian fable also illustrate this irony in their delusive phraseology with the terrible ways in which their real meaning is at last divulged and their truthfulness substantiated.

The events in the revolution of our tragedy have been reviewed in treating the discoveries, and in that connexion I attempted to show that the essential requirement of probable consecution had been fulfilled. It remains to inquire whether the moral sentiment which the imitation of a change of fortune is designed to satisfy has been recognized in the piece and illustrated after the antique manner in a discordance between the purposes of the actors and the ends really attained by them. An index to the prominent idea in the design of the poem ought to be furnished by the chorus, which officiated in ancient tragedy as impersonal promulgator of the general truths embodied by the dramatic imitation in acts of individuals; and we find, accordingly, in the lyric odes of the play passages in harmony with the tenor of the Hellenic religion. At the close of the first stasimum the chorus betrays its distrust in the new league between the hostile brothers, and animadverting upon Don Manuel's secret love and his offence against the cloister's sanctity, is reminded of the stain that rests on the princely house from a crime of the former generation: for — such are its words — the ill beginning leads to no good end; no blind chance has brought about this hate and strife between sons whose mother's bosom had been accursed, but it is a fixed necessity that every deed of mad folly beneath the sun be atoned for. * And after Don Manuel has fallen by his brother's hand the chorus, passing from its lamentation for the dead,

---

* ὅταν δὲ κρηπὶς μὴ καταβληθῇ γένους
ὀρθῶς, ἀνάγκη δυστυχεῖν τοὺς ἐκγόνους.

Eur. Herc. Fur. v. 1261.

dwells upon the retribution that awaits the author of the deed, another Orestes devoted to the avenging Furies: for although the external vestiges of foul acts — it sings — vanish speedily from the face of earth, yet is nothing really lost or annihilated which the hours working in secret ways have received in charge; but time and nature are fields where seed is sown and harvest reaped. These examples of the moral tone that pervades the choral songs will serve not only to demonstrate the concurrence of the drama with the Grecian model in the special point under consideration, but also to show that in the employment of the chorus itself the essential character of this peculiar constituent of an ancient play has been reproduced by the modern poet.

In the service of nature's retributive law those persons, as was before observed, are the direct agents, who have been condemned to suffer its penalty, and the means whereby they hasten the execution of this are the steps they take to avoid the calamities predicted in the divine warning. Laius, king of Thebes, exposes the infant Œdipus, and the prince of Messina orders his daughter to be destroyed; but the consequent ignorance of their parentage on the part of both children brings on the fate their attempted destruction was meant to hinder. Again, had the princess revealed her daughter immediately on the father's death, the girl would not have inflamed, as now, unknown to be of kindred blood, the sudden passion of Don Cesar, and the consequent fatal collision of the brothers could not have come to pass. As it was, the mother desirous first to end the feud, which had burst forth in open strife straightway upon the removal of the paternal restraint, deferred disclosure, lest the menacing oracle might come to be fulfilled, should the sister appear while the brothers were still alienated. Then, having achieved her peaceful purpose in so far as to have a day appointed for friendly meeting she holds out to the daughter a prospect of hearing her destiny declared on this day. This induces Don Manuel, through fear of a derangement of his plans, to remove the girl from the cloister, — an act which had brought her a second time under the eye of Don Cesar. Thus the reconciliation itself becomes an instrument in the hands of *Ate*. Moreover, the father had once more helped the oracular decree to fulfilment by his further exertions to make it void; holding his sons apart by force, with less wisdom than the mother shows in her conciliatory mediation, and forbidding them the use of arms in martial exercise, he had occasioned the frequent lonely hunting excursions of Don Manuel, and one of these had led the young prince to the secluded cloister. In the ancient fable the outcast Œdipus, reared in error as to his descent, when warned by Apollo that he is to kill his father and wed his mother, refrains from returning to his supposed parents in Corinth, but directing his course elsewhere, to avoid the predicted disasters, is thus brought to slay Laius and to be united to Jocasta in Thebes. And the sons of this union, born, like the brothers in Messina, to complete the atonement for a guilty disturbance of well ordered nature, illustrate in their course the same stern irony of the powers regulative of human history. Intent on escaping the estrangement invoked upon them by their father's curse they agree to hold the sovereignty of Thebes on alternate years. The possession of the sceptre engenders ambition and cupidity in Eteocles, who as the elder takes the first turn in ruling; at the end of his period he refuses to resign to Polyneices, the latter appears before the city with an army to enforce his rights, and the brothers fall by each other's hands in single combat.

Thus the religious idea upon which the significance

of a change of fortune in the Greek tragedy rested is
reproduced by the modern poet in the construction of his
plot; and the lesson conveyed in the representation of such
a history is vivified and enforced here, as with the ancients,
by employing the various forms of tragic irony. The oracle
that , in apparent contradiction of a former response,
prompts the mother to save her child , was in itself an
example of this. It is illustrated also in remarks of the
actors where they utter the truths soon to be corroborated
by their own sorrow: as when the princess in her ex-
hortation to the brothers exclaims: — Nature only is
true; she abides firm at her eternal anchorage when all
else in life drives at random on the waves. Similarly
impressive are the words which the spectator from his
better knowledge of the state of things interprets with a
literalness or seriousness not thought of by the speaker:
as when the second semichorus, left to guard Beatrice,
addresses her as a daughter * of its sovereign and as the
preserver of the royal race of Messina; or when Donna
Isabella, about to disclose her secret, says: — Hear what
was sown in former time and now is to ripen to a glad
harvest. Those passages likewise have an ironical colouring
which are marked by a glaring contrast between the joyous
sentiments uttered and the painful events shortly ensuing,
— a favourite artifice of Sophocles, in whose plays the
most cheerful odes are those immediately preceding a
calamity. Such are the choral song congratulatory of
Beatrice and Don Cesar, Don Manuel's graphic enumeration
of the ornaments to be purchased for the bride , and the
words of thankfulness expressed by Donna Isabella that
her sons have not encountered one another in their loves.

* Compare Soph. *Oed. Tyr.* v. 258, and Eur. *Iph. Taur.* v. 627.

While, on the one hand, the recognition of guilt as a cause of suffering and an observance of probability and apparent causation in the course of the action represented are requisite in tragedy, in order that a clear perception may be gained of an unfailing justice and righteous necessity in events, there is needed, on the other hand, such an imitation as will arouse in the highest degree the emotions of pity and fear; for through these emotions the tragic teachings are impressively brought home to us, and a *purification* *, in the words of Aristotle, is thereby ultimately effected in our contemplation of human calamity. With reference to this point the philosopher discusses what kinds of characters ought to be overtaken by a change of fortune in a drama, to produce the desired effect (XIII). A change from happy to unhappy, he argues, ought not to be represented as occurring to faultless characters; for this would produce disgust rather than pity or fear, being inconsistent, as I have shown, with the moral design of tragedy: nor to exceedingly bad characters; because pity arises from a perception of some unworthiness in suffering, fear from a perception of similarity to ourselves. There remains, accordingly, the character between these extremes, a person who neither excels in virtue nor becomes wretched through utter baseness, but who is ruined through some folly, like Œdipus or Thyestes, — being better than these rather than worse. The usual practice of the best poets justified the philosopher in these views: Æschylus and Sophocles did not attempt to depict abstractly perfect characters or monsters of wickedness, but even a Clytaemnestra and an Ægisthus betray enough of virtuous sentiment to claim a share of pity at their fall; if Euripides has oc-

---

* τραγῳδία . . . . δι᾽ ἐλέου καὶ φόβου περαίνουσα τὴν τῶν τοιούτων παθημάτων κάθαρσιν (VI).

casionally disregarded these requirements, it is but new evidence that this author had begun to drift away from the wonted current. The play before us complies with the rule, presenting the better grades of character rather than the worse, in accordance with the suggestion in the treatise. The princess of Messina wins esteem for her prudent views and virtuous motives, first through her address to the elders, and again in her appeal to the estranged brothers; but she betrays in both instances a quickness of temper which afterwards, on the approach of calamity, takes the form of unseemly vehemence in hasty imprecation and impious mockery. Hence the spectator, with all his commiseration for her distress, suspects that this trait may have helped to consummate her misfortunes. In the *Prometheus Bound* a bold and reckless defiance of Zeus on the part of the hero is the single instrument employed by Æschylus in reconciling the pious Greek beholder to the intense sufferings endured by the benefactor of man. King Œdipus, who claims our good will at the outset of the play of Sophocles through his benevolent zeal in the public interest, displays even sooner than Donna Isabella a defect similar to hers, in the unpardonable precipitancy with which he prejudges and condemns supposed enemies. The estimable characteristics of the brothers have been remarked upon as of a chivalrous nature and, in so far, as unantique; yet they are none the less adapted to call forth the sympathies of any audience. Their failings are represented as inherited qualities. Don Cesar's fault is a maternal one, but in the play he exhibits it rather as Creon does in the *Antigone* than like Œdipus, in persuading himself, while blinded by passion, that justice excuses the commission of an act which he afterward rues and must atone for. The offence of Don Manuel, his father's son, is like the crime of which his father had been guilty, as his excessive and fatal reserve was seen to be a paternal trait. Even Beatrice through her ruinous disregard of her lover's injunctions fails to elicit the unmixed pity her wretchedness would otherwise demand.

(c) The Calamities ($\pi\acute{\alpha}\vartheta\eta$).

The $\pi\acute{\alpha}\vartheta\eta$ of a tragedy are explained to be the destructive or painful events, such as deaths, excessive pains, and wounds (XI). They are the immediate agents in the excitation of fear and pity, — in plots whose revolutions are disastrous, through their actual occurrence, — in those of happy termination, through the expectation which they call forth of their occurrence, although they do not come to pass in fact. In considering what calamities must appear most terrible and piteous Aristotle chooses such as happen between friends (XIV), because, while in other cases the emotions are excited merely through the nature of the deed itself, in these the sensibilities are rendered more acute by a knowledge of the relations subsisting between perpetrator and sufferer. He then enumerates three ways in which an atrocious action may occur between friends or relatives: first, when it is perpetrated with full knowledge; again, when it is done in ignorance of the relationship, which is afterwards discovered; thirdly, when the deed is about to be committed unknowingly, but is prevented by a discovery. The last method, though esteemed the best by Aristotle, belongs properly to tragedies with a prosperous issue, as in the *Iphigeneia at Tauri* Orestes is saved from sacrifice at the hands of the priestess by recognizing her as his sister, and they escape together from the country with the image of the goddess: we find an illustration of it, however, in *The*

Bride of Messina. The revolting feature of the Theban story, — that of unnatural wedlock, — our poet has shunned in his imitation, yet not so completely as to deprive himself of its tragic effect. We have seen the brothers become enamoured of their unknown sister, both designing to wed her, and the elder gaining her love to this end; the spectator, therefore, experiences the dread of a calamity like the union of Œdipus with Jocasta, until it is rendered impossible not only by discoveries, but also by other events, which at the same time involve the participants in misfortune.

To commit the deed in ignorance of the relationship and afterward to discover is better, observes Aristotle, than to do it with full knowledge; for the former way is free from the repulsiveness of the latter, and the discovery is startling. The first calamity of our tragedy, — the killing of the elder by the younger brother, — though happening between relatives as recommended, cannot be classed as to manner of occurrence under any of the modes mentioned in the treatise. The deed is done knowingly, yet not deliberately like the murder of her children by Medea or Orestes' execution of Clytaemnestra, but under the influence of momentary passion. Moreover, while Don Cesar is aware of the connexion between himself and the person he slays, he is still ignorant of the mutual relationship of Beatrice to both, and hence commits an act which a knowledge of the circumstances later leads him to abhor. The action, therefore, must produce an effect upon the spectator, similar to that of one happening in entire ignorance of relations. Its atrocity is softened by the fact that it is committed under a delusion, and the discovery that makes known to the offender the true conditions of his crime is as striking as one of fraternity itself could be. When

Theseus in the *Hippolytus* dooms his son by a curse to certain death, he is aware of the relationship, but deceived concerning the youth's guilt; this renders the act less atrocious, while the discovery, when too late, of the innocence of Hippolytus is one of the tragic moments of the piece. The other calamity in the play of Schiller, forming its catastrophe, is the deliberate suicide of the guilty prince. This likewise is a case not specially considered in the treatise on poetry, but the act finds a counterpart in the *Ajax* of Sophocles, both in respect of its relations and of its perpetration on the stage before the public eye. Such a deed must be in itself more tragically moving than any yet discussed; but since the effects are largely determined by the attendant circumstances and motives, I defer the treatment of it until the remainder of the play has been reviewed.

The *exodus* opens with the entrance of Don Cesar, now in composure, while at the close of the last episodium, before the tranquilizing final stasimum, he had departed despairingly from the presence of his sister. He commands the chorus to prepare for the obsequies of the deceased prince, and his own retainers withdraw to execute the order. The first semichorus remaining reads in his words the determination he had intimated before Beatrice, to avenge upon himself his brother's death. The spectator is hereby warned that the *end* is approaching which the plot as a *whole* and as a *unit* requires. Aristotle is at pains to correct a prevalent false notion that a plot must be *one* because the hero of it is *one*, urging that many events may happen to one man which cannot be connected into a single action (VIII). He might with equal justice have warned against supposing that a plot lacks unity because the main heroes of it are *two;* for, as in this play, the fate of one hero may be supplementary to that of the other, either incident unsatisfying or unintelligible without the other, and the plot incomplete without both. The murder of Don Manuel could not form the catastrophe of the tragedy, since it occurred before all the discoveries were made, that is, before the revolution was complete. The final discovery could not give the plot its end, because instead of confirming Don Cesar's imagined justification for his act it dispelled this illusion, leaving him conscious of the guilt and aware of the necessity of expiation. His self-inflicted punishment, on the contrary, makes a conclusion beyond which the mind is not prompted to inquire; the prophecies are fulfilled, the race is extinguished, the chain of destiny broken; — τῇ νῦν ὁρμῇ τελεωθέν.*

The final scene is prolonged in a manner characteristic of the ancient stage. In describing the scene of reconciliation I was led to notice the rhetorical element, there introduced with moderation, and to censure the subtlety and frigidness that often deface argumentative passages in the Attic poetry. The eloquence of impassioned supplication illustrated in the present scene is, on the other hand, eminently appropriate to tragedy and was effectively employed by the ancients; the works of Euripides especially furnish brilliant examples of this, which, however, are often tinged with sophistry. The chorus first attempts vainly to soften Don Cesar in his determination, admonishing him, as the followers of Ajax do their lord, not to add woe to woe. The mother enters, aroused by a rumour of her son's intent, and, revoking her unnatural curse, exhausts her store of reasoning, promise, and entreaty, to overcome his conviction of the needfulness of this atone-

* Closing words in the *Electra* of Sophocles, spoken by the chorus.

ment. / Thus in the play of Sophocles Tecmessa adds her prayers to those of the chorus, and with a touching petition responds to Ajax' averment that a voluntary death can alone repair his injured honour. The mother, finding her efforts unavailing, as a last resort summons the beloved sister to conjure her brother to remain in life. In the *Hecuba* of Euripides the aged queen, after pleading vainly with Ulysses for her daughter's life, calls upon Polyxena to add her prayers; but instead of so doing the princess of Troy voluntarily offers herself for the required sacrifice. / So Beatrice, thus appealed to, unexpectedly names herself as the due expiatory offering for the dead, while she bids her brother live for their mother's sake. But when, thereupon, she evinces by word and action that she solicits in her own behalf as well, the victory promises to be with her, and the brother's stern determination seems about to fail. /

The prolongation of this scene in the manner described is adapted, like Ajax' professed change of purpose (vv. 646—692), to increase the suspense of the audience, which, reaching its highest tension at the moment of evident wavering on the part of Don Cesar, is of weight in enforcing the moral of the tragedy, since it helps to reconcile the beholder to the thrilling spectacle of the catastrophe. For this suspense is a conflict between the involuntary benevolent hope that the calamity may not occur and, on the other side, a just desire for its consummation, founded on our acquiescence with the criminal in his self-condemnatory convictions and our approbation of the leading precepts inculcated by the tragic imitation. Hence at the execution of the deed a certain *satisfaction* ($\dot{\eta}\delta ov\dot{\eta}$, XIV) of right reason is mingled with the agitating passions and finally predominates over them.

The contest between human influence and the requirements of retributive necessity is decided by a voiceless appeal from the spirit of the murdered brother. Folding doors are seen to open, exposing the interior of the chapel and the coffin resting there in state. The motives that had led Don Cesar to his resolve are thus personified and their triumph is secured by this solemn reminder at the moment of sorest temptation. The stage-device is equivalent to the *eccyclema*, by which in the Athenian theatre the result of deeds committed behind the scenes was revealed to the public view; but its application in resuing from a dilemma, though artistically and worthily carried out, suggests rather the *deus ex machina*. The worthiest example of employment of this resort to the supernatural in the extant Greek plays is similar to the present case: in the *Philoctetes* Hercules must interfere to decide a conflict between human character and divine decree, — to overcome the steadfast and indignant refusal of Philoctetes to rejoin the army that had cast him forth to perish. The guilty prince of Messina, with a word expressive of contentment at the manifestation by his sister of the affection due to kindred (the beholder requires the assurance of such a recognition on the part of Don Cesar, as he needed to be assured that Don Manuel had discovered the truth before dying), obeys the summons from the other world and ends his life with the sword. The last words, after the ancient custom, come from the chorus echoing the moral of the tragedy: —

> *The best of blessings is not life alone,*
> *The worst of evils is a guilty soul.*

The analysis of this unique drama is thus concluded. The form given to it by the poet's hand has been dissected, its parts have been separately examined and the functions explained that each performs in making up the moving force of the compact body. We can now comprehend why Aristotle calls the plot the soul of tragedy; by directing our attention upon the plot we have been enabled to glance at every vital constituent and to keep out of view unessentials, which, important as they may be to the perfection of external symmetry, were of inferior moment in the endeavour to show that the *spirit* of an extinct art had been revived. The treatment even of essentials could be but brief in a dissertation of this kind; but the analysis itself and the fact that it has been possible to unfold it upon the plan sketched by the ancient philosopher will have gone far to attest the correctness of the judgment passed. Had space permitted, minor differences and, similarities between copy and model might have been collected and weighed with favourable results. Schiller himself in his prefatory essay to the poem has called attention to some apparent inconsistencies and points of variance. He has mingled the Hellenic and Christian religions, but in such a manner as to embody the essence of the former under the latter's outward shell. He has introduced a double chorus, which appears divided against itself as actor, but which, since as ideal person it is ever a unit, violates in nowise the antique principle. Moreover, a wide participation of the chorus in the action is approved by Aristotle, who recommends this as more in the manner of Sophocles than of Euripides, — he might have added, still more after the older manner of Æschylus —; while the possibility of a partisan division is suggested by the attitude of the chorus at the close of Æschylus' Theban trilogy. He has occasionally changed the scene of the play, but this is done in two extant Greek dramas and would have occurred oftener upon the ancient stage, had the mechanical difficulties been less. Unity of *action* is a just intellectual requirement, and as such became a fixed and inviolable principle of Grecian art; but the so called unities of time and place were only casual accessories of the first, nor was the poet conscious of their existence as independent requisites. Lastly, Schiller has laid the scene of his drama in a post-hellenic period, — a venture of less boldness and greater profit, relatively considered, than would at first appear. Phrynicus and Æschylus went farther, when they repeated acts of contemporary history upon the stage; Euripides was more inconsistent, in coupling the personalities of ordinary life with the guise and stature of demigods: but our poet, who composed this work not for the antiquarian, but for auditors with hearts and souls, sought for an era that would be to *them* an heroic age, and found it in the days of chivalry.

CPSIA information can be obtained at www.ICGtesting.com
Printed in the USA
BVOW03s1425130815

413222BV00013B/62/P